Sisters, ARE YOU GETTING IT?

By Valerie Ferguson

Copyright © 2023 *vf*
VALERIE FERGUSON

All rights reserved. No part of this publication may be reproduced, distributed, or transmitted in any form or by any means, including photocopying, recording, or other electronic or mechanical methods, without the prior written permission of the publisher, except in the case of brief quotations embodied in critical reviews and certain other noncommercial uses permitted by copyright law. For permission requests, write to the publisher, Stork Publishing LLC "Attention: Permissions Coordinator," at the address below.

First printing edition 2023.

Stork Publishing LLC
700 South Boulevard Dr.
Bainbridge, Ga. 39819

www.lashawndashiree.info

In memory of my parents, Eugene & Georgianna Ferguson-Miles, in Heaven!

Thank you both, for giving me a wonderful life.

And my Step-father, Samuel Miles, in Heaven... thank you for showing my mom half of the world.

To my children, Michelle, Nicole, and Sharif... thank you for supporting and believing in me when no one else did.

To my grandchildren, Tytiana, Janiaya, Tamia, Kyheem, Mekhi, and Skyla... thank you all for helping me enjoy life.

To my brothers and sisters, Bernette, Phillip, Michele, Reggie, Gene, Lesly, and Jeffery... when y'all was teaching, I was learning!

To Reverend Phyllis White, thank you for sharing your mother, Cynthia Evans, with me. Every notebook you supplied me with gave me more reasons to write.

A special "Thank You" To "Sha".... for never letting me forget to Write!

These moments begin to feel good because it's what you really wanted, but it won't last long-term. Depending on the time and space between you two, you begin to want more. And... here you go again; you're in another worthless relationship.

Preface

Let's Take a Look

I have noticed that there are thousands of books that have been written on the art of relationships, and there are many more on the rise. There are also many new writers on this topic; some are doctors, therapists, counselors, coaches, advisors, ministers, and even celebrities. In addition to being authors, many of them also offer classes, seminars, and retreats on how to have a healthy relationship. Even with all of these available resources, I have not seen any improvements in relationships, today. Many of my Sisters are still hurting, still in pain, still unhappy, still confused, still depressed, and still wondering when they will have a chance at love and a happy life.

No, I haven't checked the statistics or researched hundreds of readers to see if any of the advice from these books worked. However, it is obvious to me that with all the research, challenges, talk-shows, and t.v.shows, on the subject of relationships there are, still, no help has been found. If a solution for broken hearts and toxic relationships had been found, the writers would be writing about success stories, not about the same old problems.

Sisters, are you getting it? That after all the books you've read, seminars you've attended, therapists and coaches you've paid…if you're reading this book, you still haven't gotten it?

Question: Are you really listening to the advice you've read from the best authors, doctors, and celebrities? Are you really being truthful in the questions you've been told to ask yourself? Were you truthful in your answers? Have you really taken heed "to tell the truth, the whole truth and nothing but the truth, so help you, God"?

STOP right there!

So help you, God!

Sisters, right there is where we have all made our mistake. We refuse to let God help us! Why is that? Most of us may not want a God-fearing man. (Thinking: He's a church man, so he's corny or boring. He wears suits. I like a thug, with jeans & sneakers. Or my favorite; I need a rough neck.) Be careful, many women that had a rough neck, got his hands on their neck and they're no longer hear to tell the story! This will be discussed later in Chapter Fatal Attraction.

Some of us probably don't believe that any still exist, but they do. If you want a good man, you must understand that he has to be a God-fearing man. Don't think that you're a failure, because you haven't met him yet. Most men don't know or believe that they can be a "God-fearing man" because they don't acknowledge that this characteristic can only be found in the word of God.

No matter which religion we practice, when we take into consideration the character of men and women, the overall teaching is based on love, and love is the opposite of hate. God is Love. 1 John 4:16 says God is Love; and he that well in love dwell in God and God in him.

The reality we all fail to see and believe is that we are all God's children. No matter how messy we are, God created us for greatness. However, we have to be willing to change from our messy ways. We must realize that we have to make some changes if we want to be seen differently. Before we move on, though, I want to make something clear. The change that you need to make is not about changing yourself for others. You have to be willing to change for yourself first! You have to do better for yourself before you can do better for someone else!

Yes, there are thousands of books written by preachers, those that are well-versed in the word of God, and those who are well-educated in various areas of theology and counseling. Yet, have you ever wondered how many of them are actually in a healthy, committed, and loving relationship with God?

So many of these books, whether spiritual or worldly, were written by someone who has been through some sort of hurt, heartache, brokenness, or traumatic experience. But the question is: How many of them have actually recovered from their own experiences?

Some of their testimonies, if they are willing to share, are coated with unrealistic truths and views that lack the substance that those who are struggling need to hear in order to break free. This is because those that have been through similar situations have not broken free themselves. They're still struggling with issues of the past, so they cannot give others the truth that will help them.

So many sisters, whether single, in and out of relationships, married, or engaged, haven't recovered from the emotional baggage from previous relationships. They have not been set free from past damage in order to start anew and give advice to others. We must remind ourselves that we don't deserve it. Yes, I had to realize this too!

Real talk... I had to realize that I had been through so much that it was time to declare, "I've had enough", which wasn't easy. I had enough of being hurt, disrespected, lonely, mad, angry, and sick.

I tried therapy, and I honestly felt that it wasn't for me. However, I learned something very important about therapy in a Christian counseling class that I attended. During this class, I learned that before we consider counseling others, we have to be sure that we don't have any personal, unresolved issues. Resolving our past trauma is necessary because it can help to avoid a drawback that may rehash repressed memories that can cause us to have a breakdown while trying to help someone else.

In other words, the only way we can help someone overcome something they are dealing with is if we become overcomers first. And sisters, this is what I believe to be the problem. I'm not trying to take away from the gratification of anyone else's success. I'm proud of those who are willing to make the effort to encourage and empower sisters. However, I don't believe you can transition from being broken-hearted one week and then write a book trying to encourage someone else the very next week. You must be careful not to take off your Band-Aid too soon. You have to make sure that you are truly free of the hurt and pain from your past experiences before trying to encourage others.

TABLE OF CONTENT

Getting a Fresh Start 14
Am I Desperate 18
Take Your Time 23
What Do I Deserve? 27
Getting What's Good! 33
Matching the Right Mate to 37
What You Believe You Deserve! 37
Word Play for Game Players - Watch the Language 41
Let it Flow by Controlling the Flow 45
Stop Frontin'! 48
(Cheatress) 53
Fighting Back 59
Tricks 66
Fatal Attractions 72

Chapter 1

Getting a Fresh Start

Let's start fresh by forgetting what we have been taught for so long about how to get over a breakup. You should start with letting go of the past, putting the blame game aside, and accepting responsibility for your own actions and what you allowed to happen. You allowed yourself to be hurt the moment you kept quiet or made excuses the stay in a toxic situation. The good news, however, is that you don't have to stay there. Consider William Shakespeare's famous quote, "To err is human."

Many people, both men and women, that I have had the opportunity to listen to, always begin by blaming themselves after a failed relationship. At some point in our lives, we all develop the "shoulda, coulda, woulda" attitude. We say things like "I should have said this", "I could have done that", or "I wish I would have found this out earlier." It really wouldn't have made a difference anyway, because if that was the person we desired to have, we wouldn't have let anything get in the way. Our focus shouldn't be limited to just getting over the relationship, we should put more energy into controlling the process of how we get over it.

How do we do that, though? First, we have to be real with ourselves and acknowledge how we are truly feeling. We often think about the person. We miss them. We're mad at them. We might even hate them, but we still miss them. One of the best ways to get over someone is to admit that although you won't get over them quickly, you can continue to live without them.

You can't get over them right away. The memories of the good times, the laughter, the romance, and the great sex, are things that you cannot shake off, especially at night. (Funny but true.) Even though the heartbreak still hurts, you have to find a way to get over them and keep living.

Yes, heartbreak is very painful. It creeps up on you like a drug craving. It hurts to the point that you want to become hateful towards the person who broke your heart. You are not only angry at the person who broke your heart, but you are also angry towards those who are connected to that person, such as family, friends, children, and their new mate; if there is one. That is your first sign of needing to let go, sisters.

Start by reminding yourself of these things daily:

1. I don't want to hurt anymore.

2. I don't want to be angry at the idea of being hurt.

3. I don't want to make that same mistake again.

Let it all go! Clothes, pictures, text messages, emails, cards, gifts, friends, music; everything connected to that person. Until you can healthily function without them, move yourself away from them, or move them away from you.

Listen! When it comes to people, you don't know everything about them, but you do know a little bit more about yourself. If you haven't taken the time to get to know yourself, like what you want or need, then you need to take some time to do the work of self-discovery! Now....Let it go!

Chapter 2

Am I Desperate?

When it comes to relationships, many of us have had our share of ups and downs. It seems like the more you try to find and keep a good mate, the more challenging it becomes, the longer it takes, and the lonelier you seem to feel. I know that "lonely" can sometimes be interpreted as an ugly word when we hear someone say it. Although we can feel lonely when we are by ourselves, there is no need to worry. It takes a while to realize that being alone is not the same as being lonely. The definition of alone means having no one present. Lonely, on the other hand, means to feel sad because you are without companions.

Here is the problem... the longer we're alone and the lonelier we get, some of us become desperate during this time. Yeah, I said it! We become desperate. Out of fear of being alone, we become desperate. We begin to settle and take what we can get. I can say that word because I have been there.

The definition of desperate is a feeling that shows or involves a hopeless sense that a situation is so bad that it is impossible to deal with.

Now that sounds bad, right? Let's simplify it.

For those who are lonely, desperate just means we don't like the feeling of being alone. Therefore, we look for a quick fix to try and cure the loneliness. Again, don't feel bad or beat yourself up about it, because you are not really alone. No matter who leaves you, God promises to never leave you. John 14: [18] I will not leave you comfortless: I will come to you

Some of those who are in relationships are lonely, too! Most people are in relationships that are dead. They are dead because there is no love, affection, or communication. They're just two people with no relation in the ship, and that's when loneliness seeps in. It stays dormant for a while until we see a different type of person that we desire. It can be something so subtle that it catches you off guard. If we are not careful, which most of us are not, we fool ourselves into thinking we can handle the feelings of attraction. We get caught off guard and begin to make silent excuses trying to find a reason to justify why we fall for this person.

For example, when we first met a man, he is very nice, you have fun with him, and he does everything right.

When we're together, he gives me everything and says all the right things. We start to get comfortable and think that everything is okay because at least we're not alone. Over time, he begins to show you his true colors but you ignore all of the red flags, because you don't want to be lonely. But after those stolen moments are over, you find yourself alone.

In the beginning, those moments don't really seem important until they start tapping on the heart. Now, ask yourself a question. Do I want to go through this again or do I want to wait for the right person to come along?

You have the choice of going through the games, hurt, heartache, shame, and loneliness again. Or you can choose to wait, by simply taking your time and having patience. Don't get tricked by the word "time" and attach the word "long" to it. It's time that allows you to see what you want and what will make you happy "long term", and not what you settle for "short term".

"Sister's, Are You Getting It?"

Chapter 3

Take Your Time

In any relationship, you will realize over time what you like and expect from your partner. As we mature, we begin to slow down and not rush in our relationships like when we were a little younger. We realize that we've made a number of mistakes in our past.

When we were younger, many of us moved from one relationship to the next so fast; quicker than we changed our underwear. We weren't in love. We were in lust and didn't know it. But, when it was over, they moved on and we did, too! Some of us were able to shake it off. I was one that "shook it off" so much that I missed out on one important thing…a relationship. I realized later on that I was a loser. I missed the important part of having a good friend, lover, and a life partner through a healthy marriage.

Then, there are those who couldn't shake their feelings off so easily. For those of us who stayed single, we moved on by letting go of the attachments. Sometimes we faked it because we didn't want to feel like a loser or failure.

But those who were attached to their partner through marriage, engagements, and children, breaking up was a little harder to do! Now if you're reading this book, guess what? You survived! You're still here. So, take your time this time. Take the time and opportunity that God has given you to make the right choices! The time we have been given is a loan. Your time is limited and is not to be wasted.

For so long, you have allowed others to control your time. Yes, you did. It started with:

1. Who they were - probably somebody else's man or into somebody else.
2. What they wanted to do - only what he wanted to do most of the things you didn't even like.
3. Where they wanted to go - places he like to go that "She" (his other woman) didn't want to do with him
4. When they wanted to see you – Out of loneliness or desperation
5. Why you were with them in the first place

You convinced yourself to believe that it was all about you when it really wasn't. Sisters, after a bad experience in a relationship, we start looking for hope in a second chance. We hope we can get it right this time. But, people can't give us a second chance. Why? Because they didn't give us the first chance. That comes from God, Our Creator. Should be a little bit left in the bowl from the last time I got one good flush.

Today, you can take control of the time. It is time to decide who you spend your time with and why, because you deserve it.

Carpe Diem - Seize the Day!
Find out what you deserve.

"Sister's, Are You Getting It?"

Chapter 4

What Do I Deserve?

Take a moment to think about the question, "what do I deserve?" Start with the first step; don't compare yourself and your relationship to anyone else. When you look at your parents, girlfriends, your pastor, and even your boss and the relationships that they all have, don't assume that it is perfect. Those couples that have been together for several years should be able to tell you that it takes a lot of work to have a successful relationship.

You must know that what they have won't make you happy. They put their own time in; good, bad, or ugly, and have their own experiences, which will be different from yours.

Firstly, what you don't see, you don't know. Secondly, most of them were, and may still be, in the same predicament as you: lonely. They may have just decided to settle. Then, there are those that have been together, but fear being in a committed relationship. They have never been married, but again, they settled for what they have.

And last but sure not least, don't let the world, including T.V., media, and books, tell you how to find the perfect mate... Not even this book! There is no such thing as perfect in anything. That's a beautiful and encouraging thought, but... nobody is perfect! All of us have flaws!

A good and healthy relationship takes true emotion and heart. Most of what is seen and read is only what we wish for and want to hear. This is how we get tricked! The best thing for us to do is hear the truth and accept it. Yes, the truth hurts, and that's why most of the time we don't want to hear it. But the truth heals and sets us free.

Most people you meet won't tell you the truth anyway. That may be because they haven't accepted truth in their own lives. William Shakespeare said, "To Thine own self be true." Again, ask yourself the question: "what do I deserve?" My answer is simple. You deserve to be happy instead of being unhappy.

Many of us have been hurt, broken, scarred, and ridiculed, which caused us to forget who we are and what we deserve. So, I want you to relax, take a deep breath, and begin to find yourself.

Sisters, you're killing yourself making your physical self over, for others. When you have to make yourself over

Mentally & Spiritually first. The people you're trying to please and gain acceptance will never be satisfied.

Ask yourself the question: Why am I making myself over physically, But I keep looking for or attracting the same type of mentally damaged mate?

Sisters....let's talk about that "Bad Body of yours that you have or trying to get. That Bad Body is Bad! Yes it is. It's getting used, disrespected, abused and it's getting you killed.

Yes, I said Mate, because some of you are meeting a mate from the same sex that's just as bad or worst as you did with the heterosexual mate.

When you Change your Mindset, you change your thoughts & actions. In changing those thoughts &actions for the good, a lot of things will begin to change for the better

Go back to a time when you were really happy in your life. A time where you can remember what it felt like to smile, or how it felt to laugh with friends and family. Can you remember being with a family member and how it felt to talk about your childhood memories? Yes, some of you may have to go all the way back to your childhood, to remember what made you smile.

Try to go back there by letting go of every negative thing said or done to you, or things you said or did to yourself. Yes, we have said and done some things to ourselves, and even allowed things to be done to us by others. Most of our pain and resentment is from our own mistakes that we have not asked forgiveness for.

Today, ask God to forgive you for mistakes that you have made, whether they are known and unknown. Thank God for bringing you through those challenges and move on!

"Sister's, Are You Getting It?"

Chapter 5

Getting What's Good!

Now, what is it that you deserve? Good question. The answer? Everything good. We all deserve to have joy, peace, and happiness. Life has its ups and downs, but none of us deserve to stay down! We deserve to have healthy mental and spiritual relationships.

A healthy "mental" relationship begins with good and positive thoughts and actions. And a healthy "spiritual" relationship begins with God word. Philippians 4:8

Today, society tries to make us think that our lives exist from something scientific, yet they cannot fully explain it through all the research they have done. they are still trying to find which came first the chicken or the egg. That's why they find themselves constantly going back to the drawing board.

My thoughts on this: If our whole life exists from something scientific, then someone had to create the scientist right?

Listen, if you want to keep your sanity, you better believe that there is a spiritual source that is higher than us, that helps us stay mentally balanced every day. You can't believe that we have all of this creation without believing in the Creator...GOD! Genesis 1:1 In the Beginning God Created...

Now I'm realizing you deserve better Christmas stop saying I'm OK yes you said it often so much that you have gotten comfortable and begin to believe it. I don't care how hot it's gotten for you your family and your relationship you're still saying I'm OK when you're not.

Do you want to be happy right? Do you want to be in love by you want to love somebody and them to love you back why do you want peace in your home right? Did admit to yourself first that you're not OK with someone lying cheating and holding you calling Dillon about who they really are in the long term agenda the cheating on you and cheating you out of being happy and as a result, there are hurting you.

In conclusion in the effort to get it was good you have to first get rid of what's bad.

Add your personal thoughts on "What Do I Deserve?" In the back of the book.

Note: Make sure you use only positive words to your personal thoughts.

Why? Because scripture reminds us that, "Whatever a man thinketh, so is he."

"Sister's, Are You Getting It?"

Chapter 6

Matching the Right Mate to What You Believe You Deserve!

Now that you know what you deserve in life, it's time to match a mate with it. For a long time, we were naive and in denial, so we accepted what was given to us. We don't have to do that anymore.

We don't have to see people through a selfish lens and create our own ideas about who they are. We have to see them for who they truly are and be able to discern if they are right for us, not only as a mate, but as a friend as well. We don't have to accept them. If they not for us, then they are not for us… It's just that simple. They may be right for someone else, but they're not right for you.

Don't settle. Do you believe that you deserve what you say you deserve? Only you know what gives you joy and peace, and what makes you happy. Some of us have become more comfortable with the things that make us miserable instead of the things that make me happy. I had to realize that in my own life, and when I did, I changed it. The funny thing about evolving is that the people that caused the misery don't even know that I changed, because I didn't change them, I changed me.

Relationships should be balanced. You must know that it's not going to be great in the beginning, but if it starts out good, at some point, both should be looking forward to growing even greater together.

Common Courtesy or Generosity

Sisters....when a gentleman offers to help....Don't say "No"....Let him do it. Then, you simply say "Thank You". Kindness is like a glass bottle. It's clear so can check to see if there is a hidden agenda. Why? Because despite what we are beginning to believe, through our messy experiences...., There are some good men left.

Sisters, we've all heard of the "Wolf in sheep's clothing, right! But, the Wolf eventually has to come from under the wool, because it gets hot!

That's like the devil. 1 Peter 5:8 says ..... Be sober, be vigilant; because your adversary the devil, as a roaring lion, walketh about, seeking whom he may devour.

The devil cannot stay nice for long, because being nice is Not his character! He is evil and that's who he is. So, when we see this character in a person, that is who he is.

So, if you are looking for a Good man…..mean, disrespectful, degrading, controlling, violent, cheating, lying one is Not for you. Because he is Evil. That is his "True" character. I don't care how fine he is. Oh, Yes he can change. But, he has to want to change for himself first, in order to be changed for you! How can he do that? He has to consult God. It's not about him getting dressed up on Sunday and going to church with you. It's going to church to make himself grow in character and in Faith, so he can be beneficial to you and everyone that you both are around. In other words, you want to look, feel and grow together! One of my favorite quotes that I wrote is:

"Never put so much time in the vision of others
that you forget your own dreams!"

Note: if they are not ready to grow, let them go

"Sister's, Are You Getting It?"

Chapter 7

Word Play for Game Players - Watch the Language

In relationships with anybody, language is a key component and the key source of communication. For example, someone that is speaking the English language will not be able to communicate clearly with someone that speaks a foreign language, unless the foreigner knows English and vise-versa. When we communicate with others in a language we don't understand, they can tell us anything and we wouldn't know the difference. The same concept applies with tricky words.

Some words can be tricky if we fall for them. Some of us have a bad habit of allowing words to trick or mislead us. This happens when our partner changes the definition of words to mean something else, just to satisfy themselves. We don't say anything about it, but instead go right along with their change of heart. As I mentioned earlier, in relationships, lack of communication will result in no relation in the ship.

For example, phrases like, "we are" and "you are" in relationships may mean different things to each individual.

a. Friends—Basic partners in the relationship, with a lot of rules and expectations.
b. Non-exclusive – Free to date other people.
c. Platonic—Believed to be attached on a spiritual and emotional level.

d. Wifey --- Not married. The woman may believe that he will marry her one day. Maybe he will or maybe he won't.

e. Hubby - the same description as wifey. Sisters the ball is in his court but know that it's not a basketball game, so don't wait on the sidelines too long.

f. Open relationship— Knowledge of the partner having sexual relationships with others. This is very dangerous. He can come back with more than he left with and you might not be able to get rid of it.

g. Sexual Partners— Physically intimate with no attachments or demands. (the same as in sample " F"on open relationship

*These are words that most often benefit one partner and not both. "I", "mine", "me", and "my", are often used by those that are selfish.

Sisters people that are selfish only think about themselves nobody else not you not the kids they don't even care about what others think. it's all about them.

"Sister's, Are You Getting It?"

Chapter 8

Let it Flow by Controlling the Flow

Don't move too fast! Things always seem great in the beginning. Yes, many have had success in a world wind relationship. But there are also those who have some horror stories.

Many people have asked whether or not a woman should propose to a man? My answer is no because I have made several mistakes when it comes to picking a man in a relationship. These mistakes came from all the things that I talked through in the previous chapters.

Another reason I would say no is because the ideals that men and women have regarding relationships differ. Women, no matter how successful she is or how broke she is; for the man she chooses, she will lower her standards. Men, on the other hand, will only settle for what they want. Especially, when it benefits him.

Note: Ladies don't get it twisted. For both men and women, it has nothing to do with money, race, or beauty. It's all about power and control.

Example: Men: It is easy for men to stay in a long-term relationship with a woman without marrying her. There are no demands for him to choose. Most women are afraid to make demands out of fear of being alone, so they settle for less.

Women: So many women have gotten destroyed by this because women think men think like them. However, most women in this position will say to themselves, "I won't get married because I don't want to." Some of you know that that's a bold face lie. (I have to laugh at this myself). If you have been in love with this man for the past 20 years, as soon as he asks, "Will you marry me?", you will excitedly say, "Yes". But, until then, you will stay in the relationship and convince yourself that you are happy. Sis, you're not just hanging on, you're dangling! What's sad about this is that he can drop you any time he wants, and the result would be heartbreaking.

I know that this hurts to hear, but we have to stop frontin' and be real with ourselves! We deserve better! (Go back to Chapter 4 for a little encouragement)

"Sister's, Are You Getting It?"

Chapter 9

Stop Frontin'!

Sisters, stop frontin'! Stop frontin' in front of others. Stop putting on airs for people who are just like you, or worse. Many of us get in front of others and want to act like everything is alright.

Let's take a look at some of our celebrity figures. One week you see them on T.V. and in magazines with their mates looking so happy like they have it all together. Then the next week, you see the same couple in the news; bruised faces from fighting, crying kids, and angry friends and family members who now have to take sides.

Stop frontin'! If there is a problem, address it. Don't be afraid. You may be living with or dating someone that doesn't respect you in or out of your home. Many of you won't let the husband lead as the bible says. The bible gives a good reason why a man should be the "Head", not just the lead.

1 Corinthians 11:3 - But I would have you know, that the head of every man is Christ; and the head of the woman is the man; and the head of Christ is God. See, It's not about money or position. When a man and woman marry, they become one... period.

Sisters, I heard a preacher tell of a conversation between him and his wife. During the discussion he attempted to express his authority as Head of the household.

And his wife reminded him that the Head, is no good without the Neck!

So, Know that You are very important in the relationship also and you are "One Body".

- Note: Any man can be the head, but the man has to be able to lead.
- In the past, even before biblical times, society set standards that were gender-based.
- When it comes to relationships, there are two types of men: a leader and a boss.
- The world says, "You're stupid – He's controlling you."

Sisters....

A Leader: A person that guides and directs another person or a group.

A Boss: To master over, dominate, or take control of another person.

You may have made the mistake of jumping into a relationship too fast. Or you may have may have chosen a particular person for all the wrong reasons. Whatever the case, there is hope at making it work, if that's what you want to do. This can only happen if the two of you are willing to make it work.

If the person you're with has a quality that you love, a quality that makes you smile at the thought of them, that may be the person for you. If other qualities blend and flow, go with it. As you go together, you should be growing together. There should be a mental and emotional balance in the relationship.

It's not going to be perfect or 100%, but I want you to imagine the relationship as a surfboard. While you're on the water, in order for you to stay on, you have to go with the flow of the water or you will fall off. Some waves in life will make you have to lean to the left and others will make you have to lean to the right. Just remember to go with the flow to you can stay afloat.

"Sister's, Are You Getting It?"

Chapter 10

(Cheatress)

I entitled this "Cheatress", because many of us have enough still cheating ourselves out of a good, healthy relationship

Sisters stop selling yourself short by thinking you are better than the next woman. Yes, many men have left their homes and settled in with another woman, but that doesn't mean he is, or was, sleeping in a bed or roses. Sisters, ask a friend or family member, "What does it take to hold and keep a man?" If they tell you the truth, you might not want to get married after all.

Sisters, first stop cheating yourself by Picking up Strangers and settling for the first pick. Some of it is trash and it don't take long to find that out.

If you don't know him or her by now, you will never know them.

When you meet a person for the first time, you only know what they tell you. No matter how good they may sound telling you about themselves, it may not be all true. The lies they tell may actually be the best parts of their character.

The truth about who they really are can be messy and destroy your life.

I'm not going to attempt to give you the amount of sisters who have died and are still being killed by these types of individuals. There were hundreds of women killed by partners of the same sex, but the number of women killed by their male partners is astronomical. Today the numbers are growing. Why is that? The reason is these "strangers" are truly strange. They are mentally disturbed, damaged, broken, angry, mad, mean, and jealous.

And you cannot change them!

When it comes to relationships, whether we want to accept it or not, age plays a major role in them. Age has a lot to do with the amount of experience, growth, and maturity we have. Just because a mate is older, this doesn't mean they are the proper mate for you. Some mates (heterosexual or same sexual partners) are stuck in the mindset of a child. Even though they're older, they can be petty, controlling, abusive, jealous, and may not have gotten over their past experiences.

The same is true with a younger mate. They may not be mature enough to handle the truth about situations you have experienced and made it through. When something like financial burdens, difficulty with an ex, or the loss of a loved one happens, you need someone that is emotionally strong to be there for you and with you.

The possibility of dating a younger person can be very appealing. They are young, fun, exciting, and sexually attractive. They may cause you to have flash backs on your younger days, giving you the desire to go back and test the waters again.

He may tell you that he likes older woman and he's was liking you since he was a kid and you are more mature than them young girls. But he should be mature enough to be willing to grow and build himself, in order to build the relationship. In the beginning you have to be strong enough to see that this man is mature or immature enough to be the man that you need and not your play thing.

Let me warn you, these young are not as dumb as you think. They can lay the smack down in the bedroom and rob you blind all at the same time, while playing on the Ps5 with your kids!

Then there are those who may have been in a long-term relationship or marriage and find this new opportunity to tempt you to want try and do those things that you missed out on in your past. Those good times your single girlfriends told you about. The banging parties and different dates they went on while you were home with the kids, cooking, cleaning, or home alone.

Sisters… real talk. Be careful. When you are testing these kinds of waters, you have to see the deep part of the pool. It's not always a shallow kiddie pool, but it can be real deep.

There are characteristics in these kinds of waters that can be very dangerous. They can include jealousy, petty, controlling ways, abusive traits (mentally and physically. Past child abuse or the abuse of drugs and alcohol), financial lack, and needing serious help. Help that your beauty or booty can fix.

Today, you're coming across many that are damaged goods and you are not in the position to "Change" or "Save" them. Only Jesus can do that! Again, these characteristics can be very dangerous and sometimes lead to death.

"Sister's, Are You Getting It?"

Chapter 11

Fighting Back

As women, we always have to fight. We've lost so many battles, but now we are fighting back and winning. Now that we are in the Empowerment Movement, we have to fight back even more. For me, it's not about winning. It's the fact that because I fought back, my opponent knows that I'm not taking it any more.

Today, it seems to me that many women are being taught that in order to fight back, they have to dress and act masculine to prove that we have power. Why is that?

Why do we have to change by putting on a t-shirt, jeans, and sneakers to fight back? Ladies, we can fight with our beauty, brains, and character. In other words, it's our looks, the way we think, and our actions that will help us win if we use them the right way.

Sisters, I'm saying this because there are going to be many moments, when you are going to have to fight back... including right now! You won't have time to braid your hair, put grease on your face, and tie up your sneakers. You're going to have a right now moment, where you will be backed in a corner, and in order to survive, you have to come out fighting. Why? Because your whole being depends on it. Your family, reputation, and relationships with others depends on it and it needs you to be a fighter.

Fighting back doesn't always mean that it will be physical. Fighting back starts Mentally with:

1. Preparation – The Way: What I would, should, or could do!

2. Spiritual - The Truth: Following Jesus. You don't want to follow those that are not leading you in the right direction. Every word written in red letters can be proven by you if you follow them.

3. Weaponry - The Life: Putting on the whole armor of God. Go to the book-The B.I.B.L.E (Basic Instructions Before Leaving Earth) says in John 14:6 I am the Way, the Truth and the Life. No one comes to the father, but by me.

You can't get in.....without Jesus!

Preparation means…"the Way" I would do, I should do, or I could do. Always prepare yourself to do something. Spiritual means – knowing, accepting, and living in the Truth. You must rely on God through Christ Jesus. Finally, your Weaponry is your BIBLE, the sword, which is the Word of Truth. Through God's word and study in the Bible you will be victorious.

Note: This is my way and was the choice I decided to make. But, from my experience, I believe that you can do a whole lot better with Him (Jesus) than you will without Him. Again, that was MY choice!

When you prepare yourself to fight back with Jesus Christ, there are benefits.

1. He is a friend that sticks closer than anyone else. You can lean and depend on Him -Proverbs 18:24 A man

that hath friends must show himself friendly, and there is a friend that sticketh closer than a brother.

2. He is a Counselor, someone to talk to that only talks back to you.

Isaiah 9:6 For to us a child is born, to us a son is given, and the government will be on his shoulders. And he will be called **Wonderful Counselor**, Mighty God, Everlasting Father, Prince of Peace

3. He is a burden bearer. He carries all the heavy loads and gives you rest.

Matthew 11:28 [28] Come unto me, all ye that labour and are heavy laden, and I will give you rest.

4. He gives you peace that passes all understanding.- Philippians 4:7 And the **peace** of God, which passeth all understanding, shall keep your hearts and minds through Christ Jesus.

5. He provides peace and security in the midst of adversity. When you prepare yourself to fight back with Jesus Christ, you can experience a peace that surpasses all understanding. In the face of trials, challenges, and uncertainties, Jesus offers a profound inner peace that cannot be explained or comprehended by human understanding.

Philippians 4:7 states, "And the peace of God, which surpasses all understanding, will guard your hearts and your minds in Christ Jesus." When you align yourself with Jesus and place your trust in Him, He bestows upon you a peace that transcends the circumstances around you. This peace acts as a shield, guarding your heart and mind from fear, anxiety, and despair.

With Jesus as your source of peace, you can find assurance and security even in the midst of chaos. He is the anchor that keeps you grounded and gives you the strength to face any situation. No matter what challenges you encounter, you can rely on His presence and His promises to bring you peace.

By fighting back with Jesus Christ, you not only gain a powerful ally but also experience the incredible benefits of His friendship, counsel, burden-bearing, and peace that surpasses understanding. These blessings provide comfort, strength, and hope as you navigate through the storms of life.

"Sister's, Are You Getting It?"

Chapter 12

Tricks

There are some people that like to play games or tricks. Some people have a way of playing on the women they are in a relationship with by using their honesty. For example, he'll say, "I'm not ready for a relationship right now!" If you are looking for a relationship, right then was the moment you were supposed to address that statement. Talk about it in the beginning so you will know whether to stay and work things out or end the conversation and let them go. Yet because they're cute, sexy, and fine, you are willing to look past that fatal flaw; the fact that they're full of it and go right into thinking that you're in a relationship with him. Their lie turns into your truth.

Tricks on Social Media Scams ya'll fall for easily.

1. Who said you need a man to pay your bills? You: "Not me! I pay all my bills" - annnnnh" (the sound of the game show buzzer)

You just told the users that You got money to pay your bills and his too!

1. How many woman can say they can take care of themselves without a man?   You; Me! I don't need a man.   You just told the users that you are home alone and they will follow you, charm you and move you right on in!

Sisters You are becoming so Independent (I don't need nobody to do nothing for me) and prideful (I don't need nobody to give me nothing) that you're letting your guards down.

These Users will come in and entertain you with a few sweet words, but Nothing in his hands. Once you start doing for that person; you'll always be taking care of them. And God forbid you wake up, smelled the coffee and try to break ties. Just like in divorce court, they feel privileged because you put them in a lifestyle that became accustomed to and you owe them.

Definition of relationship-the way in which two or more people or groups regard and behave toward each other.

In other words, when you and the other person connect (mentally, physically, and spiritually) your relationship begins. Yes, I said yours, all by yourself. But you can't see that yet! Now, when your relationship begins, the first thing you do is start checking in. You begin making yourself available whenever they want you to be available and doing what they want you to do. But these same expectations are not reciprocated. Some women allow themselves to be put into this situation by accepting to call and check in.

>*It's a trick to you, but your partner means it. They are convinced that it will work! That's why they say and do what they want to do! Usually, it works to their benefit.

People can play on your emotions if you allow them to! Men can say mean and hurtful things to you and about you with a straight face, and won't feel bad about it. This is only because you allow it and let it slide by.

But, as soon as you say one statement of truth about it or disagree and try to stop it, it strikes a nerve in them. Now, you are the meanest, evilest creature on Earth. Sisters, this can be dangerous according to the type of man you're dealing with.

Don't fall for it! Stand firm on your decisions. The truth makes change. Either he'll get it together to keep you or he won't worry about losing you. That's when you must decide whether you should stay to stay in the relationship or get out.

Finally, if you have to get out, don't be afraid to let them go! When you let them go, you let go of the mess, drama, hurt, rejection, setbacks, and misery that comes with them.

Sisters, you cannot be afraid of being alone by letting go of the wrong person in your life. Let's keep it real, no one or relationship is perfect. But, if the bad is out weighing the good, you have to let it go. Sisters, I'm sorry to tell you this, but it's the truth. The Bible says, "The truth shall make you free." It may hurt, but it will set you free.

"Sister's, Are You Getting It?"

Chapter 13

Fatal Attractions

This chapter is very serious because in the previous chapters you've read, the actions we chose can eventually lead to a sad ending. The reality here is that because of the long attractions we have attached ourselves to, there can be a fatal end. Domestic violence has been plaguing many of our relationships for generations. We are led to believe that this is a part of life. The devil is a liar and the truth is not in him, it's in God through Christ Jesus. The true words written in this book are inspired by Jesus, who is "the way, the truth and the life." (John 14:6 KJV)

Today, domestic violence is at an all-time high. There are so many sisters in situations that have them just a few steps away from death. Our sisters should not be dying at the hands of a mate that claims to love them but shows them that they really don't.

Sisters, since beginning of time, society has talked out of both sides of its face. On one side, sisters are led to believe that there are laws and provisions in place to protect women and children in domestic violence situations. Then, on the other side, sisters are overlooked, ridiculed for being in this situation, judged, blamed, left alone, and are unprotected.

Many women that are in domestic violence relationships have been in them for a long time. They have been used, abused, cheated, beaten, choked, chased, slapped, kicked, etc. After going through all the abuse and finally getting the strength to leave, all the doors begin to shut in their face. Nobody hears them, and nobody cares.

But these same people are the first ones at the crime scene to say to the media, "I told her so many times to just leave." It's sad to say, but they're right. So many of us have said these same words, and even more, to our sisters in these situations.

Fatal Attraction

"Everybody loved her!" No....Everybody don't!

When you hear stories of victims of Domestic Violence, as their friends and family members reflect on their lives, they would often say things like: She was fun, friendly. Then they would say things like: everybody loved her. She could make everybody Happy. She was the life of the party. Even if she was down, she would have positive words to say. Unfortunately, everybody didn't love her! She couldn't make everybody happy.

Chapter 3 (Take your time)

Sisters, after a bad experience in a relationship, we start looking for hope in a second chance. We hope we can get it right this time. But, people can't give us a second chance. Why? Because they didn't give us the first chance. That comes from God, Our Creator.

Until we realize this, which takes a long time, many of us stay stuck. We stay stuck because we never look to change. "Change"....is transforming our thinking from "wrong" to thinking "right".

What's "Thinking Right"? Putting the "Right" things in your mind and letting go of the "wrong" things. We all know Right from Wrong. It's just that some of the "Wrong" things feel so good! They taste, feel, smell, look, &sound good. But.... They're still Wrong?

But, we cannot turn our backs on them. Here is a true story.

In 1967 .... 37 people, Neighbors, watched a woman being attacked on the street. Assuming it was a domestic dispute, they watched the whole incident unfold, but never came outside. Never called out to the assailant. She was able to make it inside her building, screaming to her neighbors for help. The neighbors heard calling and no one came to her aid. The assailant came back, followed her into the building, raped her, stabbed her and left her for dead. And no one called the police.....until it was too late.

I believe these individuals were haunted by her death, if they're still alive.

To all my sisters, here's the truth: You have to realize that you had to make the choice of being happy. Oh yes, there is something called happiness.

"Sister's, Are You Getting It?"

From generation to generation, our sisters are being hurt and we can no longer stand by and allow this to keep happening, and believe that things can't change. Yes, they can.

How? Stop thinking a sister is stupid when she goes through somethings that you wouldn't or haven't been through! Honestly, you are just a wing and a prayer away from being a victim too! It was the Grace of God that spared you!

We have all done something stupid, in the name is Love!

When women bash, mock, ridicule, and down grade other women, by calling them out of their name, make derogatory statements It actually makes you just as bad or even worst than them.

Now that we've gotten through that…

We've covered some good ground and have cleared up some things. We've bagged up all of our garbage, and are ready to throw it out!

Now, go over the previous chapters and do a quick check up.

1. Chapter 1- Getting Started: You can do something new.
2. Chapter 2- Am I Desperate? : You don't have to be…just wait!
3. Chapter 3- Take your Time: Don't Rush… It may not be worth it.

4. Chapter 4 What Do I Deserve? : Go for what makes you happy.
5. Chapter 5- Get What's Good: There are some good ones out there.
6. Chapter 6- Matching the Right Mate to What You Deserve: You don't have to settle for less.
7. Chapter 7- Word Play for Game Players
8. Chapter 8- Let It Flow: Let it flow and let it go.
9. Chapter 9- Stop Frontin': Be real with yourself
10. Chapter 10- The Cheatress: Sisters can play games, too!
11. Chapter 11- Fighting Back: Fight back with your mind.
12. Chapter 12- Tricks: Don't fall for the tricks, you know what they are.

13. Chapter 13 Fatal Attraction: What looks good can cost you your life.

Final Thoughts

The purpose of this book is to be a strong foundation for women to stand on. There's no time for us to keep going back and forth with falling down and getting back up... only to fall again. Why? Because, we have another generation that will be following in the same pattern, and we may not get back up again.

The truth can change that! Not the truth by itself, but knowing the truth, which will set us free.

There's going to be a lot of people who get upset and who may disagree with me for writing this book, but the only ones who are going to be mad are the ones that don't want to hear, accept, and face the truth.

MEET THE AUTHOR

VALERIE FERGUSON

Valerie Ferguson, the author of the book "Sisters, Are you getting it?" is a remarkable individual with a passion for empowering women to find healthy relationships. As a Gospel minister, soloist, worship and praise leader, writer, motivational/inspirational speaker, and emcee, she brings a wealth of experience and insight to her work.

Valerie's book delves into the intricate art of relationships and emphasizes the importance of seeking God's guidance in finding lasting connections. In her view, while many authors, therapists, counselors, coaches, advisors, and even some celebrities have offered their expertise on the subject, few have truly provided a cure for the problems that countless women face. Valerie firmly believes that despite the abundance of self-help resources available, many women still struggle with emotional pain and distress.

Through "Sisters, Are you getting it?", Valerie challenges readers to confront their own truths and embrace divine intervention to overcome past hurts and embark on a journey towards healthy relationships. She recognizes that becoming an overcomer oneself is paramount before attempting to assist others in their own struggles. The book serves as a practical guide, designed to help women transcend the damages of their past and embark on a fresh start towards finding fulfilling and loving relationships.

Valerie Ferguson's ultimate goal is to aid women in cultivating a healthy, committed, and loving relationship not only with others but also with God. Her workbook, entitled "Sisters, Are you getting it? Workbook," accompanies the book, providing readers with practical exercises and activities to further enhance their personal growth and development.

With her unwavering faith and a deep understanding of the human experience, Valerie Ferguson seeks to empower women, guiding them towards a brighter future filled with authentic and meaningful connections.

Made in the USA
Middletown, DE
29 March 2024